A
Coloring
Book

A Coloring Book

Yukihide Maeshima Hartman

Hanging Loose Press
Brooklyn, New York

Published by Hanging Loose Press, 231 Wyckoff Street, Brooklyn, NY 11217. All rights reserved. No part of this book may be reproduced in any medium without the publisher's written permission, except for brief quotations in reviews.

Printed in the United States of America
10 9 8 7 6 5 4 3 2 1

Hanging Loose Press thanks the Fund for Poetry and the Literature Programs of the National Endowment for the Arts and the New York State Council on the Arts for grants in support of the publication of this book.

Some of the poems in this book originally appeared in *The World* #47 and *Out Of This World* (an anthology). The author thanks the editors of these publications and the MacDowell Colony for the time to write the poems included in this collection.

Cover art and photograph by Susan Greene

Library of Congress Cataloging-in-Publication Data

Hartman, Yuki
    A coloring book : Yukihide Maeshima Hartman.
      p. cm.
    ISBN 1-882413-27-X (cloth). — ISBN 1-882413-26-1 (paper)
    I. Title
PS3558.A714C64 1996
811'.54—dc20   95-52742
                                           CIP

 Produced at The Print Center, Inc., 225 Varick St., New York, NY 10014, a non-profit facility for literary and arts-related publications. (212) 206-8465

Contents

In New Hampshire Woods

Japanese Dreams

FLO

A Coloring Book

for Susan

In New Hampshire Woods

Pencil

With this pencil I write
where the puddles, like eyes, open,
and a book sheds its cover, and awakens.
The sun spots, flaring occasionally,
become a forest, the negative of light.
The animals, they have been up a while,
and people appear in these fresh pages
where the monuments, one by one, become.
The colors, too, with shapes and density,
and what goes darker,
what stops.
The pencil keeps writing.

The inevitable nose bleed
from too much writing and thinking.
And I thought my young heart
would never live past twenty.

On a kitchen table
a puddle of water is spreading,
and in it the neon light liquefies.
In the fractured light, a song.
The pencil is lying across the table.
The eraser, almost gone.

Another Layer of Rain

Rain comes down slowly.
A tulip is bending
in the dark hills
in the eyes you cannot see
but feel. A song takes you inside
through a forest alone
by way of fulfillment.
No one will see
and no one else has come
discovering the pleasure of knowing
in this quiet place
through some muted shadow boxing,
a fountain of new form.
No word is spoken
in frozen ember. The eyes deepen,
moist and shining, a work in progress
drizzling and misting away,
and now a splash
in the art of gentle persuasion
with a darker touch. Flowers.
How long, I dare ask,
have you been watching me?

Under A Milky Cover

In a rush of feelings. How melancholy, joy.
Guiding a cold hand to one's chest,
there seems to be more than one intention.
The eyes sparkle, chilled like ice.
This is spooky. It must be Halloween.
We join in the celebration.
Blank masks, candles and strange habits.
The wine is flowing
though the support material is long gone,
while the moon rises somewhere else
as an image is wrought, inside, and now immobile:
the pregnant pause is just too much.
There is much delay in one's misapprehension.
A false alarm is ringing,
frantically, but a telephone keeps quiet
in a pool of fluorescent light, being modern.
This is how a photogenic person is about to
become reclusive, hiding one's skeletal structure
in a safe. The combination for the lock is thrown out.
It stalls one's way of looking at form,
so much that is not quite obvious, dead or alive,
alluding to, but not pointing at, a storybook.
One by one, and in any way one chooses,
other problems surface.
Whoever has the last word, make certain
it blooms inward, and without remorse
for the feelings that it might inspire.
Beware, there is no closure.

What Comes Between Us

In encapsulating art and literature
without a proper mixture of aye and nay
between the left and the right side of the brain,
internally blooming in outward decay,
imbalance becomes our sense of balance,
while ancient worms swell up
between our breasts, giving us life and literature
where much has been pure speculation.
The angels who are broken in pieces
supply us with mad inspiration.
Vertical lines on the wall, as a sign,
released from form, become diagonal
in a form meant for something else.
In apt replacement, there is poetry.
A bell is sounding.
I answer it, with lightness of air,
though the brain works up steam,
where imbalance is working
in the questioning human eye.
This intrigues me. I plunge into the mystique
of having just declared my intentions
for no apparent reason but it sounds right.
Birds are chirping, and like a shadow,
I swim in and out of light,
which is to say, in a paradox, I am nowhere near.
In the book of riddles, looking for a place
with our lunch and refreshments,
to spread out on the grass, leaving behind
a sulking sphinx to her own devices.
We cull our wine from laughter and talk,
and our cherished prizes become less drastic.
It is time for another round of robust wine.

Notes on Dreams

for Tom Savage

He's no Abyssinian cat
but he's special
he is laden with shadows
and is lurking in the rivers.

The images come at you
from unexpected corners.
A voice from afar speaks,
and is not heard, no, not immediately.

These scissored mortals
who cut your hair in the afternoons
a kind of harpsichord's crazy notes where
baldness would be tantamount to realization.

on a hill, a rat is munching on black sun
where two roads meet, though I do not remember,
a lion is roaring at a flower.

An old man opens his mouth, in twilight,
And inside, young roses are blooming.
Some call this a trick, though
it's too early to call it anything.

It depends on what happens next.
The nature of fortunes is like this.
It is impossible to keep on laughing
without becoming a mask, a still one,
though, in laughter, everything is shattered.

You turn your face slowly, like the seasons,
where a bell is ringing, though in the flame
you are welcome. To sing or not.

A lapis lazuli door opens,
and two doves, white, fly out.
They are your eyes.

After the Rain

After a heavy shower
a pond is surrounded
by heavy autumn leaves.

We sip from this cup.
In this muted photograph
we are hidden from view
where the pond is full
my left arm around you.

The photograph is exposed
to the raw air and ruined
more obtuse more obscure.
Nothing makes sense.
Nothing is beside the point
in a love poem.

It Appears and Disappears

Facing a window, turning over a book
of magical spells, coming down to earth,
into the furrows, you spread your wings
in the dark that reveals a new corridor.
Burying your face in this misty mass,
you inhale deeply.
You refill the bloodstream
where the edges become filled with crisp tension,
taut muscles enveloping the bones underneath,
giving form to one's random observations,
contraction and release,
well chosen details,
which come zooming. Quite an aftershock.

Roasting sweet potatoes, surrounded by the aroma
of these shapes and colors, your appetite
increases, becoming dense in some,
and flamboyant in other materials:
The sheer luck of having captured
how the energy flows.
Your eyes sparkle onto the paper, then outward,
the hand moves across a sketch,
a quick flourish, it is done.
Breath is temporarily suspended
in the constraint of its revelation,
as perishables,
shades and colors,
concrete and not easily compacted,
reclaiming the energy.
Overall, referenced and deduced.
Some loose ends celebrated.
Folded, and then, cut to pieces.

The fog is lifting. The time is ripe, though
in another mode of thought, your old shell,
you shift the missing gears into action.
In the meantime, nothing happens
in slight discontinuity of brain function.
A sweet tremor is felt, and is encouraged
in the world of enlargement, where
a miniature portrait leaves indelible marks
on pure speculation, as you scurry about
among non-existent phantom making,
and the reduction theory is getting out of hand
on the verge of a crumbling tarmac
where the mechanical birds are ready to go.
The magic is working, but in reverse order,
unspooled from the book, each backward spell
eliminates the one before. And nothing remains
of the magic as you come back to life.

Kanda River

Along the Kanda River, in spring rain,
a spell is cast,
and I become moist
like a bud and bloom.

The rain comes down.

A strange ring, I hear,
that increases its velocity:
familiar, and yet dissonant.
The birds shriek in a grove,
intoning dark but sweet refrains.
The ring becomes less constrained.

A river is flowing, already.
I become pale.
I bloom out of season.

Black on Black

Spray painting black surface
with black paint
and then crisscrossing it
with black charcoal
scoring it with black pencil
trying to shoot for black humor.
I have drawn a blank.
I have this black eye.

Restaurant Review

The maitre d' has a crucified look.
The waitresses are smiling. They have had too much wine.
The angels are flying everywhere.
Like recalling in flashbacks the plump oysters
floating in a sea of cream and Riesling
who wouldn't take notice and be loved in return
for one's attentiveness to detail, the private
ambience and service, with price no consideration
eliciting unwanted remarks among the lit candles
about one's scars from the night before
listening to the music supplied on the premises
and to the point, one is required to settle down
in such a format, by degrees or in quantum leaps,
deliver what you can and be satisfied with it.
The stars, they show no drain of brightness.

Mountain Energy

for Osamu Mochizawa

What is abloom. It is beside itself.
Breaking it, and making it anew,
adding to this routine, a curious thump,
but holding onto nothing.

A special place, a special time,
breaking them down to pieces
and putting them back together
not exactly in the same way
but the same pieces.

No, not the other side, which is immaterial,
a tunnel through which so much is endured
where you see others suffer through it
in the strength of emptiness.
Under the quiet bark, under the frozen soil,
the emerald water is flowing.

To the West, the mountains,
where the sun sets, throwing
down the mountain energy.
And then a boom out of nowhere.
The East is responding.

In New Hampshire Woods

After a certain bend
in the woods,
to go deeper
becomes meaningless.
Crows, trees rubbing
old limb to new limb,
and my footsteps intruding
on my own solitude.
No demarcation
in anything.
A threshold replaced
by a path, no path.
A tree, trees, a rock, rocks.
Going down to a stream
listening to myself overflow
and climbing back up
every day, the same process.
Breakfast, lunch, dinner.
Looking out the window
past, present and future,
not so easily grasped.
Powerless, and for that
going down to the stream again
all its bubbling variations
going around, and stepping on some
boulders, lost in being
one step after another,
and feeling the spring come around
I clasp my hands in affirmation
not knowing what I confirm
but feeling stronger than ever
there must be this leap of faith
I bring all my faculties together
making the green greener, the current
more lively, and the woods more silent.
Caught between the opposing forces

of what is and what could be
I break off a branch
and swirl it around, swirl it around.
The branches come down. They come closer.
And I discover my voice. This is how I speak.

Poking Around

Easing myself down on the steps
of the Museum of Natural History
looking at two sparrows
step up to the top stair
without stirring a feather.
Tulips are almost out
in full bloom, and the vendor
under large beach umbrellas looks
incongruous as ever, and glum.
Does he miss, I wonder,
his native country, somewhere
in the Middle East
the familiar faces everywhere
the lively greetings in a language
he has a firsthand knowledge of.
Soon, it will be too hot
to sit around. The elastic and odd
logic of summer will have taken care of itself.
I give up
the spot and walk toward the park.
If you know the score
a passage from an opera might just be
floating in the soft brain
as I stare at a tropical melon
someone is carrying in her bare arm.
The juice comes splashing like a new formula.
This is promising.
Another gulp of the apple cider
under a large shade tree, off Central Park West.
What am I to imagine now
the cool air comes cascading down.

Love Poem

Some are young and earnest.
Some full of knowingness.
Being of a curious disposition,
I'm their go-between.
A certain sweetness I impart
in my sojourn as I make my rounds
carrying their packets close to my chest.
Much depends on how I fulfill my responsibilities.
I build a barrier of roses and briars
in their sleep to increase their ardor.
I take the brunt of their tender feelings.
Strange, I'm torn.
There is much that they do not see.
A delight when I least expect it.
A smile, when I deliver a message
I don't know anything about.
I look the other way to give them room
so they devour their pleasure in privacy.
Though my pleasure, too, increases,
being their guardian angel.
Some are young and earnest, as I was saying,
and some full of knowingness.
I have much to ruminate about,
playing sweet music all to myself.
I have much treasure in store for them.
Much can happen.
I experience such sweetness.
Now, I can show you this song.
Your kiss will seal it. I am certain.
The unknown, it is my sweetheart.
I love the way she moves. I'm all innocence.
Their sweet quarrel between them,
1 have nothing to do with it.
I cannot break a circle without revealing myself.
I go back and forth. Looking for justification
where none is needed. Though, if I am untrue,

who would believe you, you are not entirely safe from me.
I meddle too much in your affairs.
O, close your eyes, and never imagine.
That would be death. Better to come again and again
at my gate, where I give you all the blessings
and satisfy your desire: I am a master of invention.

I stay up nights, devising this way or that
to make a complex design look simple.
I believed too much in white magic,
too much in black magic, also, being a fool.
All the directions have reversed.
Love becomes something else. I love, therefore.
This is beautiful because it is not. It is so true.
The words can become twisted, yet not away from this.
I have much fun in confusion. I work hard at it.
I don't know what I'm saying. I wish I could say this often.

Wood

Wood softens a blow
not like steel or concrete.
It gives a little
and is no worse for it.
The resilience of its fiber is power of thought.
Hit me, and see.
Thud, thud.

New Music

In a hotel being shredded to pieces
in our central nervous system,
there is no new claustrophobia,
only old nymphomania.
I wonder if this is true in verdant Africa.
No fabulous criteria
in broken twigs from Arabia.

A teapot is tilting
its belly full of black tea.
I tilt myself up
in a tone that does not exist,
melancholy, elegant and a bit pushy.

A cassette tape
of long playing records unspools
in a form of memory loss,
where the ears become abstract,
and dangling from them, new earrings.

There is no one item
that is not contrary to itself
as a magic touch touches itself
and finds nothing there,
except new music, of course,
tapping the forbidden bars
on a piano tilting precariously.
And then, everything is divulged
as you close the book.

Thank You

You were an angel
to watch over me.
I felt it,
and for that
this small poem
as a homage
for your watchfulness.

There was this place
and we were together
a while
and together
we found a way
to be solitary.
We liked it.
Many of us, together.

It was winter
when we came.
Now, it is almost spring.
These wings, I don't know why
they beat the air
so rapidly.

We leave behind much
and bring forth
what blooms anew.
This is our consolation.
It must be so.
The wings take flight.

Big Eyes Of Chinatown

When the Big Red Eye closes,
the Big Green Eye opens.
We cross the street.
Still thinking uptown, eyeing
the not so unfamiliar vendors,
all this cheerfulness in the air
makes me nervous. Why could it not be
a bit glum, vulnerably intangible.
It is not to be.
A day for celestial gods,
a colorful parade in progress,
the dragons spitting fire
weaving through the crowd
while the Green Eye closes
and the Yellow Eye blinks.
Firecrackers explode.
I feel better now.
Munching on a Moon Cake.
Other glum people emerge
from the underground dragon stop
looking startled
about to be swallowed whole
by a paper dragon
flying above the drunken celebrants.
What big eyes they have.
Fire comes pouring down
through the thick clouds
in the form of sudden sunlight.
Another oracle has come true.
"Cloudy, with occasional chance of clearing."

Thinking Slowly

While one dissects a room in which
the infuriating magic acts cannot be interrupted,
something must be working according to plan:
analyze this formula
though not long enough to exhaust its explosive factors.
Though it is not what one wished for,
the sensation will subside in a few seconds,
sounding terrible and looking ugly,
in the act of rearranging, pure logic
and mad premise. One assumes the worst
in a philosopher's dream.
A frog is talking to a fox.
Pagan gods are walking on foot.

Japanese Dreams

Japanese Dreams

I am with a ballet company which at the present is not practicing. I am their principal dancer, though I wonder why, because I am not that young, actually quite ancient.

Because our company is not scheduling any practice session any time soon, I decide to go elsewhere, perhaps to another company. I am reprimanded for this by the ballet master: Though we are a small company, he explains, he has plenty of plans for us. If I am interested in practicing any ballet piece, he can ask another ballet master to get the score. I am an integral part of this company. I must be patient, stay with them. Practice at home.

(October 29, 1994)

Nomadic Mongols are cooking out of doors.

It is noticed that a pregnant wife amongst them must have a certain noodle dish to nourish herself and the child that she is carrying. There is none available.

This predicament is relayed to the barbarian chief who orders a huge restaurant to be erected for the purpose of preparing for the pregnant wife her favorite dish. An amazing structure is built.

I am wondering if this is not too grand a gesture. Could they not have cooked the dish and simply given it to her, instead of building such a grand restaurant in the middle of nowhere? Gold and red decorations. Dragons.

(November 2, 1994)

I find myself standing in the Realm of the Above and the Realm of the Below, simultaneously, layers of meanings and materials building up from the bottom to the top.

There are three layers of fluid matter in the Realm of the Below, and they are all made of "aliveness," the same matter that make up the Realm of the Above.

Instinctually, I realize this poses a problem. The layers below should consist of "death" material. It is too confusing, otherwise. Without a definite contrast between the Above and the Below, there is no true existence.

I change the content of the fluid matter in the realm of the Below to "death" matter, a clearer, more defined substance, in a constant state of fluidity and change.

(November 5, 1994)

I am one of four dancers. We are weaving in and out of each other, in simple and unadorned movements, each holding the stem of a flower. Each one of us represents a season. It is a dance of four seasons.

Chrysanthemum for autumn; white tubular flower for spring; iris for summer; and for winter, something red.

Each time a dancer passes by, I become aware of the intense fragrance of that flower. Especially of the spring flower, powerfully sweet, intoxicating and heady. Soon, it is replaced by the fragrance of another season. And then, another.

(November 19, 1994)

This happens some time ago in Japan.

There is a discussion in progress at a temple by a seaside. The priest at this temple is explaining to other priests gathered there that this temple is in need of a bell. But instead of requesting the bell from the heavens, where all temple bells till now have come from, he wishes for a bell that comes from the sea, that is to say, from the Devil.

Another high priest who believes otherwise is countering that point of view.

The priest who believes in the bell from the sea predicts that it will come from the sea. He prays and waits for it for years, and in the meanwhile, there are others who come to believe in his prediction.

Years pass, but no bell from the sea. The priest who has believed that the bell will come from the sea relents and agrees to a plan where a bell will be brought to this temple from inland, where it has been in storage, the temple itself having been closed for some time.

(November 25, 1994)

An old woman is relating that she has been encouraging a weatherman on the radio to venture outside to live, instead of just forecasting.

The weatherman forecasts wonderful weather, and then goes out into a fabulous day.

The old woman is happy. She too will enjoy this beautiful day.

As we walk, she peers into some bushes, to see if there are berries. She is expecting to see something yellow. But since it is still winter, they are not out yet.

Soon we come across some bushes full of big fruits that I have never seen before. They are the old woman's favorite. She gathers them in earnest. I follow her example.

They are as big as grapefruit, brown in color.

As we walk along, I see that there are plenty of these fruits, everywhere. I have an armful of them.

(December 17, 1994)

I come across a snake, which is looking for a suitable place to stay in my household. It goes here and there.

I am terrified of it. I try to chase it away, but in vain. Eventually, it comes so close to me that I begin to beat it with a stick. But it does not die. And I realize it is impossible to kill it.

After a while, I am resigned to the situation. There is nothing I can do to prevent the snake from biting me. And it does. Nothing happens to me, though.

Later, I see the snake sitting on a beautiful cushion.

(December 18, 1994)

After many years of struggle, I bring home my traveling companion, a princess, to her castle. There has been a great struggle here also. Everyone is getting ready to put the household in order.

I am eager to exchange the horrors of our experiences with the people at the castle, but the princess does not wish to dwell on it. Nor is the motherly figure and an old attendant woman at the castle. They would rather forget about the past struggle, and put more of their effort into settling into a new order.

The princess is extremely cheerful. No sign of having gone through what we have.

One of the things that must be taken care of is to build shelves in the Japanese style closets, and to fill them with knitting and sewing materials for the princess.

The order of the day seems to be to mend, and to restore. To live a life of new order.

(December 23, 1994)

I am romping in the dark, holding up a mirror, trying to discern what is reflected there. It is difficult to make out the reflections because I keep jumping around. The mirror is out of position, getting jabbed in my face as I try to align my eyes to it, but since I keep jumping around and romping, there is not a moment when the reflection can be seen clearly.

The humor of the situation does not escape me. I burst out laughing.

(December 29, 1994)

I am an apprentice to an ancient Japanese sake-making family.
There is a boy my age. I help out in making sake.

Finally, the sake is produced. There is to be a celebration ceremony on a river nearby.

Many ships bearing the name of the family are there forming a line on the river. And on them, facing the shore, are the sake masters and the local dignitaries, all dressed in blue shop coats, with white calligraphy prominently displayed on them. They are all standing up, ready to clap their hands in unison.

The senior members of the sake making family begin to pour sake into each other's glass, for the first tasting.

To my surprise, the sake master offers me his glass, which is already full, and stepping back, raises a sake bottle in the air, and shoots more sake into my glass.

He asks me to taste it. I am astonished, but do.

The sake is powerful with the spirit of the sake masters. I experience their indomitable power, and all their life experiences distilled in the sake.

It runs through my entire body, so concretely and so strongly that I feel I shall always carry this with me.

(January 19, 1995)

Postcard

From the tiled roofs of the city
where a forest stands apart
the paint on a brush is applied
where blue volcanoes rise up
and become the sky in a postcard
closer to what lies below
where shadows stay, and time passes
in a cigar box, precious junk,
and the stars are aligned closer
to the compass, and space more pregnant.
There is less clutter.
As promised earlier, this is the dream.
Thin ice breaks away
from the reverse angle of breeze.
Many things happen.
A wishing well is roaring furiously.
It is me, snoring.
Soon, it will be just morning light.
This throws me. I wonder why.

Once Melodies

Once melodies, now incense sticks,
I light a match
and set them on fire.
They smolder some,
and crumble to ash,
leaving behind them,
almost imperceptibly,
what remains of the melodies,
the sweet air.

For Nancy

The world closed in on you
and there was no way out
for you to go forward or back.
Come back, come back,
the seas and the mountains compel you.
The flowers and the vegetables that you grew,
and were proud of, they too compel. Your passions
for books, hunting, culinary art, good clothes occasionally
weren't enough to keep you here.
Nothing focused. There was no way in or out.
The joy and warmth you gave to others,
they are still here, but in another guise, unspoken.
Where you were that day, no one knew exactly.
No explanation. Except the act explains it all.
You left us suddenly, or to put it more precisely,
left your own senses, not a thing resolved by it,
except to leave open endless questions, all unanswerable.
Being alive, we keep at them, knowing full well that
nothing will bring you back.

If you should be flying about here, Nancy,
go see your cousin in Florida, go see the beloved fisherman
in Montauk, I think they need you the most.
Next, your parents, your friends, and I know nature
is always with you. You have much to do.
Being dead, you have these responsibilities.
Naturally, you must work coming to see us into your plans,
as you did that autumn night, out of the blue,
with a gift for our anniversary, ruddy-cheeked,
shy, nervous, yet strong, we thought.
That was the last we saw you, face to face,
and you were gone. It's been some time now, Nan,
and I don't know why now particularly
I think of you, and tears won't stop.
O, Nancy. Why now. Why ever. Why then.
Your gift for writing, your fears, your obsessions,

your joy. Your constructive impulses, then turned
inside out, had to finish themselves.
Philosophically speaking, any person any age
can arrive at such a conclusion.
With due respect to your person, right or wrong,
we cannot truly intrude. And this is the way.
Joy and more joy, in retrospect, you shared
with us, and kept your private demons locked
inside, flinging shut all the exits for yourself.
There was no exit. Just emptiness.
You kept smiling, somehow, until you could not.
You descended into deeper terrors.
That was long ago. Many things have passed.
You cannot imagine. Here is our report.
Susan has earned her master's in rehabilitation counseling,
works full time in that capacity down on 14th Street.
I have begun to write in earnest, again.
We haven't been back to Montauk.
We have lost touch with the Atlantic.
We haven't seen Hither Hills and beyond.
Napeague Road is now just a memory.
Many people we knew through you
we have lost touch with, partly because you are not there, not
    anywhere,
but mainly because we have not yet come around
to making peace with the irreparable damage.
You keep coming back. And you bring with you
those who you loved and cherished.
You bring us together, little by little.
This is your responsibility.
You have heard it all, by now, I'm sure.
In a way, we looked to you, as that lighthouse
in the harbor, and felt comfort in your steady beacon.
You blinked, and it seemed all darkness.
The light is still strong in Montauk.
The waves still pound.
The fishing boats still go out at the crack of dawn.
Nothing stopped for you, Nancy,

just those who loved you, and were loved by you:
as the song goes, so goes this poem for beloved Nan.

P.S. Our cat says hello, she's 18 years old
this week. It is like being ninety in human terms.
In many ways, she's more than human, we think.
Being not so well, she eats only fresh fish.
She likes sole and scrod. Steamed in microwave oven.
I think that you'd think this is funny.
We still talk to you in this way,
and not too infrequently: it gives us solace.
And sometimes, with a smile, we salute you:
the young fisherwoman of Montauk. The superb gardener.
A good friend. A dear, dear Nancy of many faces.
We have much to catch up with. Come, time and again.
In emptiness there is no more room.

Breeze

for Vyt Bakaitus

A breeze,
the sound of it
rushing through the tall trees.
Minuscule to minute, and then to gigantic;
what is invisible.

Under a rock, the soil is moist,
and on top, it's a breeze.

A road through
a tunnel of straight pines,
another kind of energy.
Closing in, and parting away.

What remains there
under what condition
what nonsense. Deeper,
then what again.
Keeping in touch
with what passes.
Enough
to know it, and know well.
Rounding it,
leaving no trace behind.

Speaking in tongues
not so easily understood.
What opens before you.
No direct translation.
What again.
The unheard of.

Morning Raga

Waddling side to side
On a slight incline
Kind of absentminded...
The long shadow of a man on a bike
Flat on the concrete.
The morning sun blasting on trash cans.

Dog

A dog is sniffing
His own piss
And then barking
Arf, arf.
Poker-faced.

A Coloring Book

Where One Stands

For the pursuer and the pursued,
each pleasure is new diffidence,
just as the right and the left
reverse themselves completely
by simply crossing a median line.
A new perspective is thinking
(how out of context it used to be)
as the context is adjusted
and the dimensions given new looks
and the fractions rounded off
just so there would be an ending
to begin with. How utterly ridiculous
going backward from the conclusion
to its inception, finding many crooked
reasons why this does not work.
If you run amok in a sweet circle
eventually you arrive stupefied
just around the corner, out of breath.
What a chaste soul you are,
and what extravagant debauchery.
This does not make sense.
Taking a position, slightly off center,
keeping the argument going,
you step to the side, and tilt it,
and give it a spin,
each time something goes right.

Epilogue

A chain that is broken
becomes a halo, and the halo
that is too bright is a chain,
as when the one who chases me
to the end of the world to capture me
could become my dinner. The chain and the halo and I
as a threesome, chattering animatedly
as our conversation becomes a momentum
at one point in time. Finally,
we carry the unfinished business over
to the next cycle of halo, chain and I.
A new attitude is discerned
while a measuring stick is applied
and a piece of wood is marked for a new form
before its time. The chain has become the halo.
What is the difference?
One can deconstruct anything.
The chain is looking at the halo
with trepidation. They must become closer,
in the meanwhile. This is done,
going after it like a sumo wrestler.
The contest between heaven and earth
is continuous. No one winner is announced.
Though one loses face quite often.

Idle Talk

In the milk of life
I would like to be a stick
that stirs it, while my dreams precede me,
in my aura, like fracture,
and also in my persona, which strains,
as each new profile is supine,
swarthy and in the dark.
Though one never consummates completely
its reverse movement, one is compelled backward.

Other melancholy things happen
as I wonder why
in high intensity light,
much power is being drained
and a bolt of lightning
illuminates a deep gash
across a piece of paper
in timbre of sweetness.
Like a beheaded torso, a sample of beauty,
so much that is amiss,
can be left to imagination,
and there is also
artful talk in theological studies.

So the true cost of being alive is
how, from itself, it is deduced
in my secondhand impressions
like observing the pouring rain
and being soaked through with one's recollections,
which is slightly different
from actually having been catapulted into attention
when least expected. How fast the whiplash.

Dreams of life are less simple now
as life demands an immediate review.
My delaying tactics seem to have become antiquarian,
and in a library, stacked to the ceiling,
a blizzard of unread books and papers,
— become lost in my private misgivings,
and my archivist seems to have fallen asleep
while my dreams edge closer to a precipice
which is how I come to, unable to fathom
that my study period has come to an end
and it is time to play, in sweet estrangement
from my work ethic, without striking a pose;
there is an intermission where I am a mere bystander,
ponderous like tropical flowers, slowly ripening.

Conceit of such art is simply dazzling
in a spatial relationship
between the things that are incompatible,
not in the name of immediate reconciliation
but in hibernation, apart from conjugal kisses.
One allows for the space to be occupied
by the time invested in idleness, that, in time
bears curious fruits, and rising to the occasion,
one is pulled downward by sweet earth,
its nose freckled with youth and wisdom,
in the shaded eye, in the heart that is empty
of enmity. A hand keeps writing,
before the final curtain, or penultimate to ecstasy;
a quiet moment, one becomes thoughtful,
opening a line for another turn at life
in a composition. Breath and gorgeous rhythm.

Poem

So much distance breathes in a pencil
On the white paper... with a faint shadow.
Having traveled the millenniums in one step,
The distance is you, emerging from a moment before,
And you bend down to pick up the pencil
Repeating your foreboding as notion of reality.
Backward or forward, the liquid solutions ripen.
And out of them come transparent shadows
Catching you peering down from the sheer height
And you yield to the splitting sky like the clouds.
You move on, which is reflected in luminous ripples of the mirror.
The surface of steel grey pouring out of nowhere.

Chalk

for Lorna Smedman

It's brand new, though
A long time.
Lorna, and her lakes.
Or, spilling coffee on the table.
I think of you when I think of literature
Seriously and there is a special commentary
Section that I noticed yesterday.
Did you read it. It mentions your name
In relation to American Lit. before
My time, really, who was that
Who taught at the Ferris School for Women?
Did I tell you also I noticed
Your brand of dedication and style
In re-telling a history that no one
So far has said not in the same way
You phrase it backward and forward
Distilling what has become for you
A vision, and then no more diddling
With a closed case. No, nothing is
Closed. Ever. That is how you open
Your lecture. A long, lazy afternoon
Of study, and pleasure, of reading
And of dreaming in concrete terms
Putting the pieces back together not in the way
You found them; naturally, that would be
Illicit. I can imagine you using that
Word not to mean morality in the flesh
But to mean something more logical
To extract from the word its core
Not what it appears to be saying
And yet that would be okay too ;
Clarify, and you are lost. Don't,
You are dead wrong again. Interesting.
You lift chalk, draw something in the air
And in the way you ascribe to the tone
Of your voice, stability and momentum, it becomes clear

What you mean. You mean back to square
One. And by way of a circle.
And not without morning and afternoon
Coffee and cake and laughter. Plenty of
Laughter and seriousness. The chalk
Against the blackboard. Your mind at rest.
No, not at rest. Suspended in literature.

New Trace Material

These might be what you are after, as summer crowns
asparagus and arugula, tomato and nightshade,
swollen eyelids, black coffee, bright and yellow eggs:
in subtle strokes of pencil along the surface,
powder, color, shadow, perfume and accentuation
hurled onto blank space, marked with borderlines
of your artful daze, my love, a discarded tube of mascara
perpendicular to the shadows amassed on it.
Closer to my eardrums I hear earthquakes,
in and of themselves, where a ceremonial knife is displayed
beside a tablet of fragmentary titles and stories,
two pectoral disks, turtle pendants, funerary masks,
and a nose ornament for a sedentary person
who is coughing up sunlight before his nascent demise.
Crocodile-Headed Beauty, Bat-Headed Beauty, Elephant-Headed
    Beauty,
who lift your body into the pyre of their knowing eyes,
they will, with unexpected sudden pauses, intone
in the next breath how a sodden target is raised,
and a ball of clay splattered against its surface,
as you write, each image lifted from the inkwell,
then hammered with mallet, and deformed into shape:
the golden masks are laughing, in their own restraint.

At A Museum

In the unfinished business,
two crowns of white hair,
not far from truth serum,
just missing the mark,
in time for our heated skin,
when we are out of breath
in the next breath,
sparked and forestalling
a story that has no meaning
in a box of old photos,
where the breath heaves
as 'to seem reckless
within the boundary of art,'
out of time in fragments,
out of sync with the typewriter,
but germane to what is going on
like salt grains on a bagel
smeared with cream cheese
with slices of sweet onion,
a can of cream soda, besides.
Cool enough on a hot afternoon,
spooky in the ice sculpture,
with slices of elegant lemon,
where the objects of art
melt away from the waist down,
exhausting the old imprints
as the rapture of rooted reflections,
for, like tannin in the tea,
the tongue is tied in many hybrid notes,
a book is full of shapely deconstruction,
chilled to its maximum capacity.
In the museum after hours,
there is nothing else:
one's odd nakedness,
one's incongruous private parts,
the wide-open pupils,

the ear straining for the slightest allure of a rustle,
the mouth about to spill the most intimate details,
in effect,
keeping hidden what is visible to all,
encrusted from the outside,
but fluid inside.

Untouched Part of Anatomical Studies

For the life of a reader,
there is much that is gradual
in hydrating one's thirst
knowing where to go
with no thought of sex
munching on cookies
sipping warm milk
reading alone and quietly
hoping for a prolonged pleasure
in retaining one's attention to the end
that thumps and skips a beat
with secret places of the heart
each stroke granted with leisure
of unbroken play: so it is with poetry,
as sex is to many people
a new anatomy lesson
in uncharted waters
as I wash my mouth with soap
(not unlike a cat's saliva
on the tongue rolled over his fur
how thick and shiny his coat);
how unfinished my story,
there is no more roll
of film left in my eye,
except some dimly lit halls
that remain like a box
of old photographs
left untouched since the last nightmare
of a daytime soap opera
that comes into my view. Chattering my teeth
before an intangible horror film
that reminds me of midsummer night's dream
I swallow my own words of molten iron.
In all the pictures taken till now,
I wonder aloud if this is how I know
why my age remains the same,
and why is there so much clutter
while I grow old and do not remain.

The Natives Are Laughing

On stilts and wearing whitecaps,
as the waves come in,
current value is deducted
from what is said beforehand
as form, wet hair and its still flow,
its law of averages as ball and chain
and convention are arrived at.
One is free to compound
the problem of bloom
in slow speed of twilight,
and a nap taken on hard surface,
(an arm folded under the head),
a new compass, all four limbs
sinking into still life,
its perfume, its charm,
like dark tattoos of youth
with white blotches of sunlight
if you come to think of it
all glaze and laughter,
a shift in perspective,
twisted like a towel
and turned inward across the page,
which would be just right
off the pages of some despicable poetry magazine.
If you will stay with me, my anchor is already hoisted,
bidding good-bye to my previous mode,
which, like a baboon, is babbling on the beach,
beating my chest, which is no longer there
but here with me rather astounded:
for there to be perpetual vocal contortions,
there has to be perpetuity and tongue
that is asynchronous with what I am doing
with this piece: crumpling it into a ball
and throwing it in a trash bin, which hums
vibrantly, well done and well conceived;
rigor mortis sets in beautifully.

In case I am called to testify later
on behalf of my other half in icon demolishing,
I mark the spot with a piece of tape,
while making sure to leave much in serious doubt,
to be kinder to my sense of justice,
content that I am ahead of myself by a strong nose,
which throws me, severing the base of my thought,
while, from afar, I am simply amazed
that so much remains theoretically inconclusive.
Rats. They carry on. Gnawing at the nose.

I Too Can Explain

While starfish and lobsters construct in the brain
a new mathematical equation, I sway my upper torso
in the seaweed of more recent composition
that inches up the printer drum, allowing myself space,
blinking and emitting noise,
simulating a song parallel to the vocal inflection,
but as I go along, much can change, and does,
asking more questions, in the third person singular:
Should one take more remedial courses this summer,
while one's hips become a literary commotion
on the page, toward the vertebrae of stillness,
in place of a previous model, and I aspire for a jolt
of new experimentation, each of my nerves rearranged
on a negative, where the words too must connote another pitch.
Easily, one can be caught napping
if the thread is weak in a web of intricate thought.
While one snores away and betrays no false emotion,
honey is collected, and the sweet catacomb built,
and, through a hole in the argument, the drunken bees.

Hoisted Chairs

In between the contorted lines,
closer to the end of a story as it erupts
naturally, it is the next day
when one reaches it:
in any other circumstance,
innocent bystanders are sloughed off,
secure in the knowledge that
the one who is doing the sloughing is beyond reproach.
What sophistry. I control my urge to be hysterical.
This is wanton knowledge.

And to the point, new languages are being born
in the metronome of blood, which is music,
where, from a little body of knowledge,
much excess blood is spilled,
not as devises of art, but for pure artifice,
drawing daggers from my crumpled poses
under ice and snow, a cluster of chives.

I like this drawbridge,
made of red brick and timber.
Crossing it, between involuntary convulsions,
then only for a while, I smolder
on the back of a donkey,
in all the time that is not there.
My internal clock sinks deeper.
Spring is here.
O, it is time for my medication.

Naturally, the best part of the rotten meat
cannot be edited out. If one knows at all
what dirty work this is.
Irony makes its presence known
when a good ending avails itself.
The blue sky is winking
among magnets and flowers, open for interpretation.

Where chairs are hoisted on tables
upside down, a picture comes into view:
the winter's barrier lies there
broken, bleeding fresh daffodils.
In the meanwhile, a carafe is waiting
to be emptied of wine, to be replaced
with more wine, one's thirst is now expounded.

Unhinged, there is no more pretext,
the crosscurrent suddenly is rolling,
not for the future itself,
but for the undelineated chapters,
a fool's random voyage into the time zone,
where the scrutinizing eye never sleeps.
I feel slightly noxious
in the two hemispheres called the brain,
now that the form is in place,
twisted in a thought that does not stay:
I must lie bare and be counted.

Where the bathing beauties parade past in the dark,
one leg on top of the other, from the edge,
the corners stiffen, but the book is very light.
One tip, it comes tumbling open.
No one seems to mind
if surgery is being performed
on a heart that is very removed.

In a book full of trailing pauses,
connecting the dots
to draw a picture, there is a problem
in the sequencing order;
a dorsal fin can be seen circling,
while an underwater compass cracks in two
and the fin seems to turn stiffer.
The threshold begins to shake noticeably.

A bird cage is filled with strong odor,
as the brain comes to rest
on a grass pillow, soaked with heavy dew,
structuring words with a broken mechanism,
backtracking one's dormancy, thinking how odd:
as counterfeit money buys real things sometimes,
emotions too can induce a sense of truthfulness.
The tea is much too steeped.
The book is left open in pouring rain
while the hemline is lowered, and the neckline
plunges, as I down my cool martini on a wet afternoon.

Another catacomb comes to life, a brand new house,
flexible this time, like snake patterns on the sand,
which is the nature of time, dissonant,
and in between the pauses, music is composed
in minor keys, but it is out of date,
and out of time. Delirious, finally.
Which is to say, one begins in earnest.
A wish is not to wish it.
A seamless scene is molded out of mangled parts.

I have a bad cold today--
cranky but this is for you,
assaying pajamas for you, two pairs,
striped red and cheerful
like the grey sky:
my mood swings
back to the warm kitchen at home
what a miserable day
rain and cold
cross-dressing like a blue umbrella
under the drip drip
of a sentimental journey
washing my mouth with soap
and the seam is showing.

What could go wrong: everything.
One keeps erasing the slate clean.
A bell is ringing.
I had completely forgotten
The alarm was set for afterlife.
The day zooms up, a new prizefighter.
A jab to the right, an uppercut
to a face slightly averted
in a mirror. A real wake-up call —
what a champ, suddenly undone, released:
the hand is steady
while the foundation is tilting.

A Coloring Book

Dark circles under your eyes
a sure sign that something indeed
has taken place in the meanwhile;
thinking, making love, nonstop, to the words,
until we fall down exhausted.
What a strange flower arrangement.
A crisp page. Blank and possibility.
This could be a beginning of coloring in
what is yet undetermined, before I am finished.

Wincing, I should take care of it,
but I keep stalling
in my frivolous life
that revives like narcolepsy
by unfamiliar word association.
Thinking about it, suddenly
in my inert hands there is much time,
while all my bright ideas die
and an enigma grows younger
under the gaze of a Sphinx.
The young seem to know.
They grow taller.

Primrose and icy water,
fever and rapid pulses
in these strangled pieces,
okay this will do
nothing is ever perfect
a grudging acceptance
in a bottle of ancient wine
the unending chemical reaction
it makes you think
where it is too fleshed out
the bones might show
with rouge and eye shadow,
as if to descend,

blood-soaked in life's pool,
onto the page, exposing the ascending interior.

A delicate piece.
It opens
when spoken to
and it flows like gasoline
and ignites the eyes.

It is shaping up nicely
in a circle of chalk
where I used to play dead
in a deepening trauma,
a shell is opening and closing,
while someone like me is crying.
And, as suddenly, simple solutions
breeze through, and that is that.

Think again, and this time,
depicting a scene of vivid immersion
while your heart goes on plunging
deeper than expected, and longer,
the less said the better.
A coloring book seems to keep extrapolating.

An insinuating theory
in a steady flow of words, each holding onto
the one before, fearful of being separated
grammatically, before their usage becomes explicit.
What a strange rat race. Each rat glistens beautifully.
Watchful owls stand by, with sharpened talons.

Shadowboxing blithely and hitting the mark
every now and then, black and blue
from telling too much that is not true,
bursting at the seams, trying to keep a straight face.
What makes one laugh softly.
Someone is crying in the next century.

Repudiating what I had believed earlier,
this is simply not an option.
I like this explanation.
While the hand is writing
and the eyes are reading,
the book stands upside down
with the motion of wishful thinking
instead of counterpointing
fashionable manners of speech: I should
parrot as best I can this thundering heartbeat.

The service entrance is closed today.
I enter the premises on another pretext,
through a photograph taken long ago,
where the rain would be drizzling
steaming like a loaf of fresh bread,
on anonymous streets, in cafés and bookstores,
each page full of life already lived.
Turn to page one. Erase all viable clues.

Oysters are shucked, and on ice,
chilled just so, with delicious hot sauce,
chunky pieces of tomato and horseradish.
Washing it all down with vodka and tonic,
with beer on the side, as the summer comes
sauntering back, half his shirt undone
in torrid heat, and his untidy manners
invite disparate things to come together
like a triple-decker sandwich. The clouds
drift in cumulatively. Chilly and grey.

Slowly, the things I don't quite understand
become useful to me, indirectly speaking
of nightly spires: a dream could drop exhausted
on a rumpled pillow. Your hair comes tumbling down.
Validating these words and pictures, a storyteller
on a bird tail is flying away, screeching.

If one presumes to think, I cannot fathom
there is more than one false thought
in early morning meditation. There are more.
The eyes become limpid, and the lips know
where to go. I feel like a debutante,
but without the glaring gap
between expectation and circumstance.
The details seem to become a sum of lesser considerations.

From the expression of screaming agonies
to that of smiling serenity
a long time lapse,
and, shivering, a goddess is showing her breasts,
geometric and awesome,
in a gradual chemical decomposition
of brain matter. A figure stands in the shadows,
holding back her pearly laughter.
Naked deities stand on top of each other.
The picture is too convoluted.
A giant eraser is brought in, though
no one is audacious enough
to use it, for fear of erasing oneself.

Nailing shut a coffin, and breaking out of it
as if from a bad sleep, this is too labor-
intensive. Bottom fishing, catching no bottom fish,
having to apologize, and not really knowing
why. Another metaphor might work better,
for instance a book of poems
with no cover, the blank
spine soiled with repeated use
for a purpose not intended.
A lovely cover story.
I roll my baby eyes.
Roller-Derbying around a dinner table, chasing after
my reluctant muse. The room begins to spin.

Live music and free beer.
The reception afterwards.
This notes a special star.
What a beguiling story book.
Reading it, one becomes slightly nauseous.
This changes everything.

Be back at four-thirty.
Gone for art books
that you would love to have,
what a pesky crowd, and in mid-afternoon
this weekday city, too, the very books
I have been calling for
all over the city right before me,
for you, really, drawing and painting
to your heart's content, I hope.
I rest my umbrella in the hallway.
The paper towel soaks up
all signs of what has taken place
till now. A dry package on the table.

Hello, a reptile with beautiful skin
comes to study my bone structure like an X ray,
each shade a nocturnal sublimation
of the senses, unspoken but understood.
Moisture and motion, gleaming and dark,
to cast a spell. I linger a while longer.

Byzantine chants on the radio,
and then jazz, all morning. Mona
Lisa, not too mysteriously overdrawn
in a song. Doodling, on the floor,
crayons of many lengths and colors
scattered among the forgotten pages.

Other muted circumstances converge
on this one, and my problem is sequestered
in a first aid station. Scruffy angels hurry about,
hypodermic needles in their hands,

somewhat crazed by emergency routines.
A small hand on a clock face moves a bit
as an afterthought. A sense of irony
taps me on the shoulder, while a vicious
cycle encircles me. I am impressed.

What would it be like
to play a part in a flashback, as a live person'?
not because you are alive again,
but to be among loved ones
in another guise, not retroactively
in a mortal thought, and not as something that,
like writing, in new velocity, flourishes.
A magnesium flash goes off, smoothing the break
between here and there.

Unspooling a tapestry to its origin, you may find
that there is still some warmth left
in emptiness that smells of musty embraces.
A pair of hands is working away
in a story to find a continuing thread.
In a shoe box, a goblin is sitting alone
where tears seem to have become rust
on a fading icon. And the kissing
in autumn colors becomes more subdued.
A redundant signpost is thrown out the window.
Throwing I Ching with defunct coins,
one smiles ambiguously
as the crux of the matter is crumbling away.
I put the reference materials aside.
There is no lack of wine till the early morning hours.
The head aches slowly.
This is one demerit.
A dog would be barking
on and off, as if remembering to bark.

In the construct of spring action,
a concentric circle loosens its grip
and becomes a spiral, sliding across
a mathematical equation in neutral space.
If only I can read this holograph properly,
I could resurface as a real image.

"Quick, quick and slow, then dip,"
a shady lady is whispering to herself.
A deer is peering out from a postcard, curiously.
The sea is pounding.
On a sheer cliff, I stare down at a cove below,
somewhat bewildered, in a gentle breeze.

The coffee is percolating nicely
in passive disorientation. No strain shows.
From time to time this happens to everyone,
as one teacup is talking to another teacup,
and if they are full, they spill over.
A blue skirt is blushing.
Each broken hinge is flying off.
A new installment has arrived, finally.

The quiet seems to be a precondition
before one forms an idea
in a temple of thought, where iguanas are pointing
their heads in different directions, and are adamant.
Brownie and coffee.
Something camp and lighthearted.
This coffee-table edition contains
more than it can possibly say. Looking at it
askance, there is some disengagement.

A complex web of intrigue is spinning
a simple diagram, while I lick and taste
white caramel of clouds,
cotton candy on a day at the beach,
descending the esophagus.
A hefty encyclopedia is dropped

on the other foot. With downcast eyes, a shy
acknowledgment, one comes closer to the edge
and is failing. And far away, inside,
a diagram is drawn of body sensations.

The loose ends come tie me up
in a form made of insubstantial material.
Trussed up, stuffed with what makes me
somewhat postmodern, left in an oven
at 350° I wonder if I am cooked
and become juicy before my time.
Dreaming and wondering if I am really here.
No wonder, I am pink and fresh.
There are pinch marks all over my body.

The harder one tries to climb out, the deeper
the pit becomes. Can you still hear me?
I backtrack to an arbitrary date, where I was born,
which is time, and into the depth of the calendar,
disappear, and being incalculable, I feel free to
digress, pros and cons weighed tacitly,
the fulcrum in motion. I feel queasy.

A dark blue rug is flowing through my slow dream.
I sit on it, letting my mind wander
in the forest of blue shapes, until
something sharp rises in me, and keeps quiet
for fear of appearing to be too resolute.
Much that goes by the wayside is coming back.
There is to be no sequel.

If this magic act is to be a success,
I had better become more deceptive.
A hat trick is suspended
while I work on my dedication to true magic.
My assistant is parading in her swimsuit, smiling
like a new leaf. She is too peripheral.
I wonder if we are fooling anyone yet.

Without a doubt, I am risking my neck to be broken
if I continue in this vein. Better not
insult your intelligence. I bite my tongue.

A school of bright fish is swimming across
a steady flow of words while a typewriter is tapping
raindrops on a page. The wet spots become swollen
with fiber and ink, and streaks
of coffee stains and biscuit crumbs.
It grows darker.
The typewriter keeps tapping.

The impact of the keys awakens the words on paper.
The coloring book is much maligned.
A rabbit pulls me out of a hat.
The magician is dead, and he looks at peace.
My ears have grown quite long, and my nose,
a wooden peg. My eyes are a charcoal drawing.
Though two dimensional, I seem to be breathing.
The moving picture rewinds to the start.
This time, substitute a noun for a verb.